Historical Etchings

TRAVEL

Copyright-free illustrations for lovers of history

Compiled by
Bobbie Kalman

 Crabtree Publishing Company

Historical Etchings Series

In 19th-century North America, hundreds of artists produced black-and-white steel-plate and woodcut engravings for newspapers, periodicals, books, and catalogs. Over a period of more than five years, Bobbie Kalman and Peter Crabtree traveled to libraries throughout North America to research these etchings for Crabtree Publishing Company's *Early Settler Life* series. Researching etchings meant working in climate-controlled rooms to make sure the pages of the old newspapers and books in which these etchings appeared did not crumble due to age and dryness. Special photographers had to be hired and approved.

Many of the etchings in the *Early Settler Life* series have never appeared in other collections, so Bobbie is often asked for permission to use them. By popular demand, they have been gathered into a series of their own: the *Historical Etchings* series. Today, although many of the original sources and creators' names are forgotten, these illustrations offer a fascinating glimpse into the daily lives of the settlers of North America.

Crabtree Publishing Company

350 Fifth Avenue	360 York Road, RR 4	73 Lime Walk
Suite 3308	Niagara-on-the-Lake	Headington
New York	Ontario, Canada	Oxford OX3 7AD
N.Y. 10118	L0S 1J0	United Kingdom

Cataloging in Publication Data

Kalman, Bobbie
   Travel: copyright-free illustrations for lovers of history

(Historical etchings)

ISBN 0-86505-916-0 (pbk.)
This book contains etchings and accompanying text depicting various modes of transportation in the past, including boats, sleighs, coaches, railroads, and even horseless carriages.

1. Transportation—History—Juvenile literature.
[1. Transportation—History.] I. Title. II. Series: Kalman, Bobbie. Historical etchings.

TA1149.T74 1997   j388'.09   LC 97-37456
                                                       CIP

CONTENTS

Thousands of people came from Europe to North America in the 1800s. As many as two thousand people crowded aboard each ship. They endured terrible conditions at sea to make a better life for themselves in the New World.

Most immigrants to North America sailed in cold, dirty cargo ships. The travelers received very little food, and many were ill by the time they arrived. They slept in tiny bunks that were shared by as many as six people. Many passengers preferred to spend their time on deck, where the air was fresh.

People built canals to link bodies of water such as lakes and rivers. A system of locks was made to raise or lower ships so that they would be on the same level as the lake they were entering. This ship will be lowered as the water drains from the lock.

Many people used horse power to pull their boats through the canals. Once they went through the lock and reached a lake, they unhitched the horse and either sailed or rowed their boat.

In some places, ferry boats took people, carts, and wagons across a river or lake. This boat was attached to a rope and was operated with a system of pulleys. The boat in the background is a steamboat. Traveling by steamboat became popular near the middle of the nineteenth century.

Steamboats offered their passengers a comfortable voyage, entertainment, and good food.

Traveling by sleigh was the best way to get from place to place in winter. The jingling bells attached to the harnesses helped make the ride fun and warned pedestrians and other sleighs to look out.

People traveled more during the winter because they had a lot of free time. City streets were congested with sleighs, horses, and pedestrians as many rural families enjoyed a getaway from their farms.

Cutters were small sleighs drawn by a single horse. Sometimes people drove too quickly, causing the cutter to tip and spill its passengers onto the snow.

People loved to go "dashing through the snow" on their sleigh, but they did not necessarily arrive faster. They often lost control of their sleigh on the slippery ice and snow, so accidents were very common.

A farmer and his children attempt to clear a country lane with an old-fashioned snowplow.

Travel in the wilderness was much easier in winter than during the rest of the year. Sleighs could glide easily over the snow, which blanketed the mud, ruts, bumps, and tree roots that hindered wagons in other seasons.

Passengers crowded onto a horse-drawn coach to tour the countryside. The ride was bumpy, but the sights were a pleasant change from those seen in the towns and cities.

The mail coach drove on wheels during most of the year but, in winter, its wheels were replaced by runners. The coach carried passengers as well as mail from town to town.

Stagecoaches often carried money from one bank to another. There was always the threat of a robbery during a trip. These bandits knew the route the coach would take and ambushed it on its way into town.

This lone bandit planned to rob the coach, but the passenger inside surprised him with plans of his own!

The settlers in this Conestoga wagon have stopped to rest. Their wagon provides shelter and carries most of the supplies the family will need to build a new home and farm on the frontier.

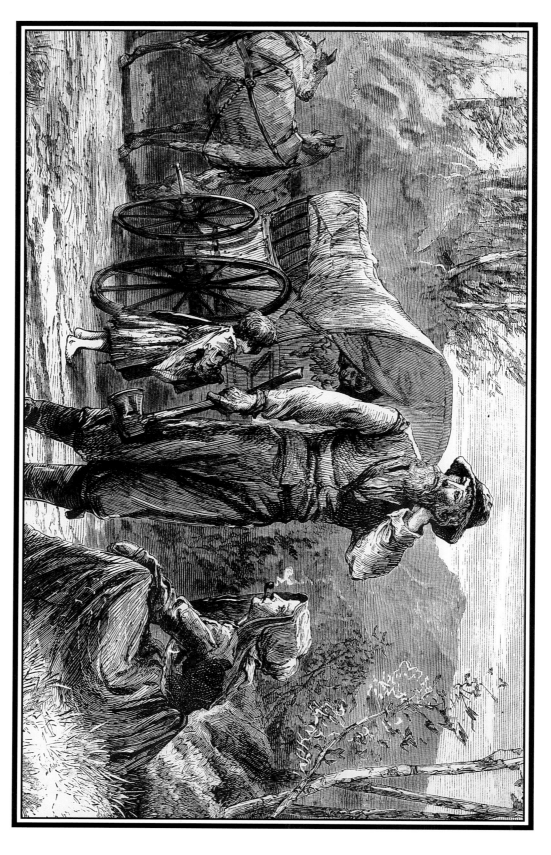

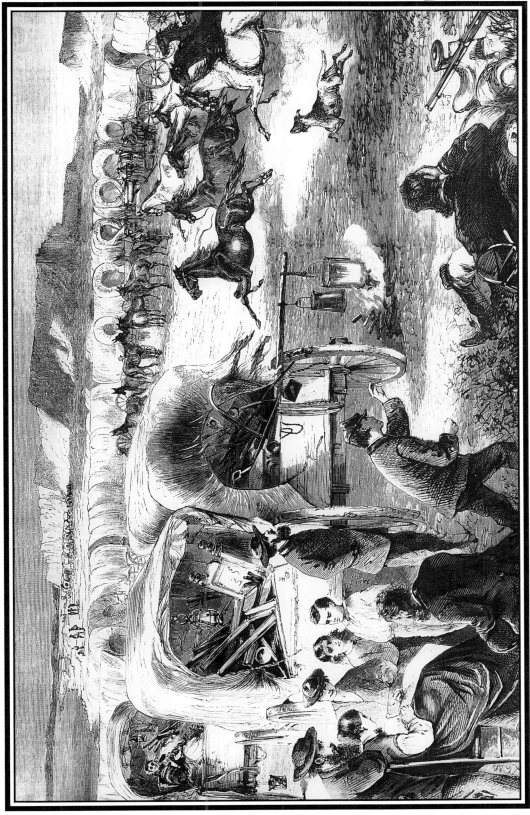

Pioneers heading west often traveled together in long wagon trains. When they stopped for the night, people arranged their wagons in a tight circle and camped inside it. The wagons protected them from attacks.

When there was no bridge or ferry, travelers often had to ford a river or stream. The horses were reluctant to cross through rough waters.

The farmer's cart was indispensable. With it, a farmer hauled rocks, wood, supplies, crops, and even his family. Horses or oxen drew the cart.

On Sunday afternoons, people went for carriage rides. The horses were groomed, the carriages were carefully polished, and the passengers wore their "Sunday best." Fashionable women carried parasols to prevent their skin from tanning. Those who were on foot stood by and watched the procession.

A runaway wagon was one of the perils of land travel. If a horse was spooked by a loud noise or another animal, it sometimes took off and would not stop. A group of people, holding hands, formed a chain and stood in the path of the horse. The sight of the human barrier often stopped the runaway horse.

Before the railroad, mail was transported from town to town in coaches. People received their letters much faster once the mail was carried by rail. This mail pouch will be picked up by the train that is passing through town.

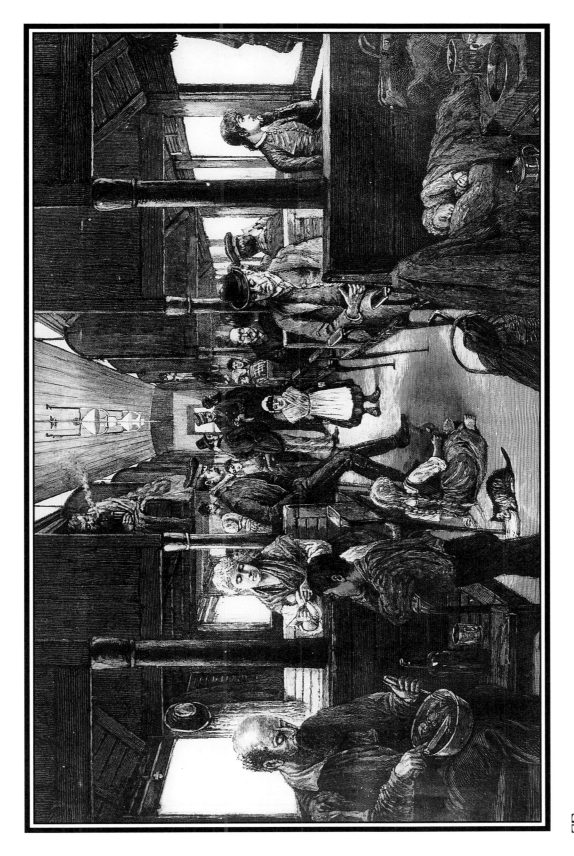

This train is carrying immigrants to their new homes in the West. The railroad joined the east and west and made it possible to transport people and goods more easily. Wherever the railroad went, new towns quickly grew around it.

he conductor had to watch the tracks ahead to make sure there was nothing blocking the train. It looks like there's trouble ahead of this one!

Sometimes a mistake was made, and trains traveled towards each other on the same track. The conductor could not stop the train in time to avoid this crash!

Early streetcars, drawn by teams of horses, were a popular method of travel in the cities. Eventually they were replaced by streetcars on tracks.

These early commuters are riding bicycles called velocipedes. Velocipede means "fast walker." Many people used them to travel short distances in a town or city.

People were very proud of owning a "horseless carriage," but these new cars needed gasoline, which was not always available. This driver is happy to see the peddler in his horse-drawn carriage. He has gasoline for sale!